The Flagpole Dance

The Flagpole Dance

poems by

Jerry McGuire

Acknowledgments

Some of the poems included in this volume were first published in periodicals as follows:

The Bad Henry Review: "Getting On/Empty Set"
Connecticut River Review: "Souls Above Doubt"
Convorbiri Literare (Romania): "Valentine," "Mole," "Watching Her Sleep"
Cronica (Romania): "Ballet for Two Ears," "Cultivate and Make Music," "Three Animals"
Earthwise Literary Calendar: "Springsong for my Parents"
Escarpments: "Jonestown 1," "Jonestown 2," "Them: Fragments," "Big Shot in his Head"
Familia (Romania): "Two Hands"
Great River Review: "Gus"
New York Quarterly: "Late Talk"
Out of Step: "Make," "Ventriloquist," "From Buffalo," "Old Man in a Wheelchair, Waiting"
Painted Bride Quarterly: "Rio Bravo"
Swift Kick: "For the Baby," "Spring Frogs in Late Winter"

Cover art by Don Pardue

Design by Christopher Howell

Library of Congress Cataloging in Publication Data
McGuire, Jerry.
The Flagpole–Dance
P. cm.
ISBN 0-89924-070-4
I. Title.
PS3563.C368344F5 1990
811'.54 — dc20 90-6487

Lynx House Press books are distributed by Small Press Distribution, 1814 San Pablo Avenue, Berkeley, California 94702; and also by Bookslinger, 502 North Prior Avenue, St. Paul, Minnesota 55104.

Lynx House Press, Box 640, Amherst, Mass. 01004

CONTENTS

I. Still, Black, and Dry

II. The Price We Pay

III. Valentine

I

Still, Black, and Dry

The Edges

for Susan

In Providence, tonight, and in Connecticut,
they are tracing out the margins of the eye,
or are they verges, they are emptying
the soul of an English bulldog puppy
into a slow loris. They intend to observe
the transaction.   And measure it.

Your sleep is so eager, I envy it.
Hardly anything breathes so much
like a dead man, as this night.
I could run to the refrigerator
but the faces of my mother and father
are in there waiting. Better never to eat.

Two men attained to an Himalayan peak,
having eaten a third climber. Then they touched
each other's cheeks, and they were sweating tenderly.
I might pretend, for you, that the edges
of everything are secure, for instance,
that this appearance of fog on the town is "just me."

Two Hands

Squirrels at night come tapping, go
ticking off, little late risers

whose toenails are typewriters
methodically scratching while my own hands

return themselves, one stone
and one bird, the bloody string

of the body stretched between,
and the squirrels' irregular incisions,

red-eyed rimshots along the nervous
edges, tied bird of night

and stone of night, pair of night
criers, tangled up and strung up

up too late strung out laid out along
the long string of duplicitous instants:

and would you take off if you could?
and would you stop it, heavy hands, cut

that skitter and hop, stone bird, across
the sharp lines of the roof's edges and risk

never again hearing anything at all, even
your own frighted pulse of repetition?

Rio Bravo

Go ahead, say it!
John Wayne

You wuz wrong, Mr. Dunson.
Walter Brennan

About the color of the river.
About its shape and name.
Wrong about the odor of
cattle
coming off the river.
Wrong for being so
blue-nose sure of yourself
myself in on under
the river. And about the kinds
of fish in that river. The
parasites in on after
the fish. The
wolf
that wants them all.

As for the drive
I'll set my mark on it
shaped like the river.
A man's mark,
bloated burro
a rattlesnake hit.
Under my sign my cattle
our your cattle
will wind and flow to
Abilene Saint Loo Wichita.
All those cattlefish
floating off bleaching
beside the rapids.
Those dreary ships our buckboards

Those dreary ships our buckboards
lunging up the waterfalls.
To spawn in Abilene.
My sign a lunatic bull
bobbing like an apple
in a tin tub
in Wichita.
And now you tell me
at this particular bend
I was wrong.

The Three Animals

Two men met where three roads cross. One held in his hands a kitchen sink. The other cut out his eyes to have it. There at the crossroads lay the blindman, squirming in his blood and making noise.

What a racket bounced among the branches of the nearby trees! Some of it was names, name of the father, name of the mother, name upon name for the anonymous cutter. And perched in the highest branch of the nearest maple was a blackbird, elegant prince of mimics in the neighborhood.

Down upon the poor man writhing in the dirt returned his own list of proper names and curses. So intensely came his babble back to him that he fell quite still, as if between utterance and echo lay a healing mystery, the secret of replacement that every word is. He sat up straight, in fact, and strained to hear, and thought, or thought he thought, he heard the blackbird promise or begin to promise that later he would give him back an eye.

And that is when the bird stopped literally dead, gobbled in mid-chatter by the kingsnake, hiss hiss hiss. The kingsnake went to sleep for seven days and dreamt of singing gaily to the blind-man, who now, seated in the road, screaming "finish it, finish it!" was set upon by humming iridescent hornets intoxicated with the perfume of his blood. The moral: it does not pay to love too dear the sounds of your own voice. Nor should one travel in inhuman company. Nor come without one's senses to heights of hope or expectation.

Jonestown: 1: *Punishment*

For breaking creed, you dig
in a circle
around the outside
of the farm
and you can't talk
to no one
and you got to say
over and over
My *evil make me break creed*
My *evil make me break creed*
My *evil make me break creed*
My *evil make me break creed*
and the sound
ease your muscles
so they don't ache
a real miracle
My *evil make me*
the sound your voice
over and over mix
with the digging sound
and together they say
right back at you
My *evil make me break creed*
till you don't want to stop
want to just keep
digging that circle
deeper and deeper
round and around
you dig and pray that way
and you look up and see
you're putting the farm
way up on a mountain.

Jonestown: 2: *Escapee*

Green leaf
hopper yellow
snake is you
poison? Going

to eat

that hopper?
Not going to
eat me mister
yellow snake is you

just passing

through like me?

Is you always

stuck here
inside this hole
in the jungle
hunting for hoppers
where a little
light shines

through is you?

Is you dead

set on little
hopper friend
is you cyanide
man in this circle
of sun

you boss here
mister yellow
mister yellow snake

you the one

in charge of putting
out the lights here?

(S)he Said

I feel that
the brown oasis
of your   strange

being is in fact
the backbone
hollow   and burnished
like a painted nail

of the harp
that shudders up
the wordless cantata of the universe

he said

I think
that a strange thing to think
but this
is really the way we are

Rapes: A Ballet For Two Ears

Three smooth boys mount two lean white horses.
Loving their mothers they shine in the moonlight.
Two bright willows tremble together.
The heavy legs measure the sap moving through them.
Everything echoes the deep-voiced silence.
Four pale studs mount the smooth-flanked children.
All of the haunches glow and flutter.
In the still black pasture nothing is listening.
Red-lidded villages blink their answer.
Mothers are praying, their voices growling.
Deeper and deeper the woods are humming.
Higher and higher the trees are whistling.
The boys are screaming, the boys are screaming.
The pasture is dancing. The horses are listening.

The Flagpole Dance

Every time he does the flagpole dance
all the little multicolored kids
come bopping to the sidewalk,
hoping for balloons. Sometimes
pennies as from heaven drop, one time
showers of flowers. He wobbles on a ball
no bigger than the earth
that squats in the center of
Mrs. Maginnis's fifth- and sixth-grade classroom.
Under his lurch and pause, it turns
spacious as a cinemascope ballroom
and THE COPS CAN'T GET HIM DOWN
TILL HE WANT TO COME DOWN.
HE STAY UP THERE LONG AS HE FEEL
LIKE DOIN' IT. *(he aint scared no fuckin' cop.)*
They do come, too, their bullhorns cowed,
hands limp on their wallflower hips,
all heads cocked like sunflowers towards the source,
while he does the flagpole dance again.
He's scared shitless, and they know it,
having seen him tremble and sweat
after touching down a dozen times before.
That's what gets their goats!
he tells the kids, when they waltz
bashful to his park bench gaping:
They can't stand a man that's scared
to dance and keeps on dancing!

Poem

It is all thin wires, thin wires with you,
quick burn, dust, ash, high pulses, thin wires
sustaining intricate leaves on hasty trees
traced with crazily tender precision
along every margin and the borders
of this town aren't safe with you,
the sweatshops, the childfuck motels,
the imaginary horses prancing like blue glass
through the arty streets with you,
wrapped in thin wires, the Christmas trees crackle,
the tinsel is lit and glitters in a niagara
of lousy amateur poems chasing you
like yappy dogs, there are rivulets
of moonlight on thin wires, walking
thin wires across the gorge, the gorge
rises tonight on thin wires and we are seen,
they never spot the thin wires we fly with,
the lenses   the shutters   the strobes
suspend us like light children dancing
on tinsel strung in the air, thin wires burn us bright,
the leaves are leaving in gilt flutter,
the children sit agape, wondering under,
thin wires, thin wires, snapping leaves,
quick burn and ashes, ashes, all fall,
down of intricate geese, blue, honking
on the next street over tonight you will see
an unbelievable sight, an orphanage
burning thin wires, high, high pulses,
the children will sing unseen tonight
under a rash of cheap and obvious stars
until the invisible wires under everything
have gnawed out the roots from under anything that shines

for Gail Fischer

The Rest Of You

The one under the matchbook
has kept count while the rest of you
were sleeping. The one under
the one under the matchbook
has kept sleeping while   the rest of you
don't count.
                                        Now here's a guy
walking in small circles in a gleamy mall
while all the rest of us are dreaming
of moving in those circles that delight us.
The lights are brighter than us all,
singly or together, whether we're off or on.
And on and on, off he goes in circles,
while the mall turns incandescent
like a runway under a map of stars
towards which in perfect linear descent
a 747 is approaching while its passengers
watch "I Led Three Lives" and fail to notice
that their lives are ticking off like a clock of stars
except for that one insistent figure
in the wing-seat by the window fingering
his matchbook. He reads: "Success
Without College!" He doesn't read the rest,
as the rest of you go on not moving,
moving towards the runway, towards
the evening's bright display of shoe stores
laid beneath you, a thousand Christmas people
motionlessly spinning under the mall of stars.

From Buffalo

for Jim McGuire, 1928-1978

Went to see my brother tonight
had his once-big body upright
in a special chair, the back
cocked forward just enough
to keep his lungs in touch
with some pretense of air,
and his legs, puffed up from sugar
and cracked from lack of use, pouring sap,
were jutting out, laid across another chair.
His eyes came up like lemons
on a slot machine and didn't
know me. He coughed red
till green stuff spewed from his nose.
I said   no I didn't.
The doctor came and plugged
him in. "Every hour on the hour,"
chirped the nurse. Laid
a cup across his nose,
poked his arm with a cold needle
and hooked a hose up to his throat.
The sounds came echoing out of him
like horses dying slowly and in pain.
His eyes turned up again wishing
me gone, and without a blink
shifted to the eyes of a young man
who threw me in his '53 Buick
and took me to a pine grove
where all that blazing afternoon
he hurled whiskey down his throat
and he and his amazing friends
told jokes about the Bishop
and the Actress and there

for the first time I caught
the meaning of a joke   a break in pain
a pair of eyes with the laugh
stuck in them after the laughing's done
scent of pine grove
stuck in a white room
after the laughing's done   long done
went to see my brother dying
in Connecticut   no   yes   I didn't go.

At Praise-Time

Never easier to sever the words
from the lips, tongue from heart,
never crisper to feel the douring pulse
(if songs came from engines we would hear them still
as lilting things of the machine's soul),
this was the same innocence for a while
as the time of that whole warm city-full
of mothers under the orchis-moon of morning
bundling off the little ones
for the special bus, the *Zodiac*,
the polyseme, while over the cradled hills,
the glazed sun lurched to find the easiest signs
biased in a cryptologue of hyacinths.

Weatherman

Barry says beautiful skies
tomorrow. That means
snow. Or mudslides.
So? . . . So. On the Big Map
you can see the centers turning
and Locally, see here, where
the Lake Effect powders
the face of our area. Barry says
from our Weather Satellite
the Twin Cities will be
twinkling under an aura
of translucent rainbow-frost.
He comments on the stars,
a flurry of dancing bees.
His eyes hop away, our
High Pressure Front is being
carried away by wind-gypsies.
Trickle of sweat down the forehead
of the Southern Tier. Hint
of a tremble in the Interior.
Atop the power-towers
guarding our perimeter
something like dazzles
are dowsing, dipping after
the green stuff under the grey stuff.
Barry blushes. The sun, he says,
will be stomping like a sailor
on a midnight shoreline faggot.
A cloud will be over us all, you know.
He says the Mountainous Regions
will be cool tonight, and distant,
his map flat and dull
over his shoulder, looking at the red dot
on the lens of the machine
that keeps him crosshaired for the
little man in jodhpurs who stares away
at a woman framed soundproof
under glass. So? Barry beams.

Staged Whisper

It came that the round globe
of her face shattered in sunlight
at the beam of our small ship,
its light sail dancing, and nothing
could have shaken down the tears
of the sky's hard laughing from the lean,
supple pole that she had cut, stripped,
cured, and tooled herself. I could
have breathed swordfish! Everything
was one brilliant baby's bubble
reflecting everything else, and behind
it, a smile. Only the darker water,
cracked by the bow and left befoamed,
whispered in a prompter's mastered hiss:
listen to me, there is no hope:
opposite the vulgar lies the mandarin:
the scars on the blue water cry out:
even the gulls see you and are diffident.

It Will

It will unfold like so many cutout paper soldiers
come round and meet itself in its own womb

It will find itself wandered in way deeper than it ever goes
whistle in the dark stare at the stalactites

It will   it will go down in the hole by itself
and drive him out with his eyes bugged out and his tongue hung
        out

It will overwind all the clocks to stop at 8:20.
It will perch on them each for the length of its desire

It will always find a way. When it finds one
it will toss it away and find another way

It will eat itself and find in itself the oily spoiled taste
of the brat who went to sea to come back dashed against the
        rocks

Black Night

O you are big, big, and I
am whatever the beneath of big is,
and I beneath the big and bound
to it am big as well for being
stuck moveless in the face
of it, in your face. And I
cast no shadow against the shadow
of you: I am *that which has no shadow!*
I am a fire hydrant in August high noon
that some drunk has unplugged
for some kids. Some sun up over
us all. Some cop trying to keep
his black shiny shoes dry. The drunk
dangles his big wrench, toughs out the cop
to the kids' delight, but he's ready to *be off*:
he throws no shadow in the flood,
under this sun all is dark, black
night, gushing into itself in wet
implosion, flood of everything that disappears
into itself, the hole beneath the big
beneath that is Beneath itself:

Let us lie, let us lie, let us lie
beneath each other, still, black, and dry.

II

The Price We Pay

The Mole

The sirens are miaowing
and she says
what images do you see
in the dark and I say
scotch plaid no
a Navaho rug
a hawk big purple hawk
has a bear in his claws flying
with a yellow bear in his claws
the bear
has a badger in his claws
the badger has a coon in his claws
coon has skunk in his claws
skunk has squirrel
squirrel rat
rat mouse
the mouse has a mole
in his claws the mole
has a man in his claws
the man
has a hawk in his claws
big purple hawk
ok? She says
ok.

Late Talk

listen he said
the stars are humming and
the cuckoo clock
went off just then and
why why why
is that a question
is that really a question
or a stupid answer
she said and
the toilet flushed
and if it means
that much he said
we can
and then the garbagemen
came and took the garbage
and she said
please just a little
bit would help
won't you try and
blip
bleep
blup went the sink and
god damn it he said
something always gets in the way

Watching Her Sleep

Her lids locusts
            her pupils ripe grapes
her lips vibrating
            leading the column
of muscles and nerves
            and brain
out into the dark
            the tongue teasing
lingers over a dry crack
            saliva glistening
over the skin, now the thing slides
            for its own moist sake
the mouth now opening
            like a well full of promises
            like a hole
in a shotgunned deer
                                    the body
a palimpsest of gestures
            sometimes meaning   something
                                                (tic, tic, tic
in the lid)
            as a heavy blanket
sometimes means
                        bad weather

3 A. M.

In the night's belly
the dog growls
to go outside and piss
the room upends
cold air licks me naked
at the window
I watch him weave about
ruining every bush
he wash my sleep away
washes
I have eyes again
to see my nakedness
here in the kitchen
at three in the morning
it's god damn cold
he's picking the back yard
for a dead squirrel
I'll kill him
I'll kill him
but he's padding back
he's back
the night's tucked in
and we proceed
back to the wide-eyed bed
I stare at the hole
that purrs before me
creeping through the dark
until it steadies
breathing stilly above me
permits the images
that permit me sleep
trees like rocks
wind like water
sea like birds

Gunsmoke: An Aubade

As our forces uncouple
and you retreat
from me
rolling bellydown
into the far foothills
of the high mound
of blankets,
the flowered sheet
rolls with you
clinging to your roundness,
clefts and flank
like wine-sweet dew.
Behind me, the relentless line
of indians and rustlers
scorches my earth.
Puffs of smoke,
pockets of hell-fire
rise and pulse.
Yet you roll from me:
I holler after you:
"Wait for me! Wait for me!"
I follow like a hobbled horse.

Big Shot Of His Head

1. The Maze

We show the little ones. Here is our hearth. Here is our cupboard, where the cups are boarded up. This is the insignia of a dead plumber, sunk now in his own juices. That is the sky, we think. Along this wall, icons. We could walk through here and over a bridge, down along a curved smooth chrome corridor for a long held breath, left at the third crossing, right at the first after that, the Anacoluthon, down a rope ladder, through the middle of the Three Oracles, with their tentacles, over the hilly path crossed twice with barbed wire fences, through a room with many red, amber, and blue lights blinking, down the first hall on the left, then the fourth on the right, and through the broad yellow doors. If by mistake we pass through the curtains, instead, a tall, serious black man will be saying, almost softly singing, "Put up your bright swords, or the dew will rust them," but if we rightly choose the yellow doors, we will enter a plastic bubble, a big one, where the Houston Astros will be engaged with the Los Angeles Dodgers. A man named J. R. Richard will be pitching. There are some who say, "This is from the 19th Century," and the rest hold their stomachs as if they were laughing about cramps. Sometimes the little ones show us, the faint runes written low down on the walls. Here, "Elmer's Glue-All * Strong * Safe * America's Favorite Glue *" and here, "Zig-Zag * Braunstein Freres * France * 78 Papers * " and here, "That these meanings are not always isolable is evidenced by the fact that function words, or such unique morphemes as the *cran-* in *cranberry*, are difficult to define. Even these, however, can be known by contrast. *In* is not *through* and *cranberry* is not *blueberry*." In fact, no one understands that one, how "in" is not "through," when we are always moving through what we are in, when we live in what we go through.

2. A Certain Short Party

The gang is singing. The gang is singing: I'll be glad when you're dead, you rascal you. Nothing captures the untruth of the moment like solicitude. Emmet walked toward the wall. When he got there, he realized that he would have to stop, hit the wall, or move in some other direction, left, right, back, or up. Beneath him, there was the floor. This made the crickets in his mind jackrabbit like leapfrogs. Great artists, he realized, had since the gloomy morning of recorded time recorded time. Something said, Ny-Tol, and chimes went into his head until the very National Guard armories danced. Bottles and bottles of Perrier water! Baubles, bangles, bright shiny beads. ring-a-ling-a. Someone is knocking. Someone is ringing. Someone is ringing and knocking.

3. The Wall

Sometimes—when I think—You—the quiet Absolute—the desert object blushing green—muted looking past—the inevitable Great Mistake—fogging all the panes—peripherally I'll notice in some—corner of the room—a breath of pale motes whirling—where the sun—informs the wall—O I will sit there—flying—like a wren—who—from her nest—is taken—by a twist of storm—and hurtled—past your eyes

Souls Above Doubt

They shall return
More than they were,
And ever ascending.
Emerson, "*Give All to Love*"

Stately loops the monumental day on itself frozen in an accident of no diminution, everywhere one sound, a simple pulse that cuts itself, but plainly. This is not a day to dare to grow away from. And if the moonfaced morning spits on us, that is its promise, greened in the hot glass houses of The Irish Question, of South Africa, of State Castration—flowering murder in bloom on the morning lawns. Then we will go fishing. Behind my father's house, down the hill, skirt the berry-brambles and watch the broken bottles. We will grow younger as we descend. Down by the water we will be green as children, afraid of our bait, and the mysteries of the fat bullheads will appear to us as so many whiskered fatalities, already fading to grey, fading to nothing.

Gus

I

Her great failing was only a certain shrillness that came in when she felt her will shaken. Her failing was not, was never a failure of will, was no kind of backing down at all, not ever, not even against him and his overpowering willfulness. Only that, when he'd come in after sawing wood all morning, out in the snow and cold, his crooked right index finger hairless and cherried with its steel center holding it in its perpetual interrogative, when he'd come in exaggerating that old limp of his, either from cold or meanness or from want of love, and the filthy puddles of sawdust-crudded melt remained like a careless signature where she'd spent all morning mopping, then she could hear, now that the children were gone into merely courteous adulthood, she could hear her own words come hammering out between the walls he'd straightened when she'd asked him to, after they'd been buckled for twenty-five years, her words reverberated about the place until it seemed as though some awful actress from Secret Storm or Love of Life were overacting her part, until she wanted to say, or at least to think, that's not me, that's someone else, even while she knew it was herself, and so still felt that old cocoon of shame magicking itself around her, numbing her a little closer to being dead, probably for good.

II

Sometimes now when she played solitaire between 8:00 and 10:00 in the evening, when she dozed between hands, she let herself flutter around among ideas she'd never countenanced before. One that she dreamed that she dreamed often involved a parallel existence. Not an earlier one—in her alternative life she felt a sort of partner, and she believed that something like telepathy was involved. She felt herself lying in an enforced silence, night after night, beside a lover who wrote stories and poems in a brown notebook, by an amber light. Often, for his self-absorption was so perfect that she could see all that he wrote, and he never noticed or felt her breath or knew the approaches and withdrawals of her spirit from him, she would see that her name had fallen on his page, or a description of her eyes, puffy and pale, or an anecdote of a woman who waddled like a duck when she walked, a woman who had waddled right out of her best years and into this strange life of solitaire and yes, it was she, not the young woman dreaming on the bed, who turned up in the brown notebook, and she would look at the old man, attendant upon the tv, and he would rarely, very rarely, look up at her, his eyes making no reference to the grotesque spectacle of her bulbous, grasshopper eyes, and he would ask her if she thought she felt like making him an egg sandwich.

for my mother

An Open Letter

THERE WAS A GIRL who was sustained by sustenance itself. She discovered that the agony of imagining herself became an adjunct of a diary, the echo of an adolescent fuck-story.

Forty superficial horsemen had she tendering her kitchen-maids. Into hot furnaces cool would they ride at the nod of her grinning head. No one told *her* what to do!

Even the forty boys guarding her swimming-pool stayed through the evening when their day-shifts were through. Fat colonels stalked through the property. Peacocks sang, both live and recorded. Snakes on the wires of their tongues played melodies, snails sang harmony, all was as delicate as a bucket of frogs' eyes.

She didn't care!
She didn't care!
She didn't care!
She didn't care!

That's what they said when the milkmaids complained that the governor's lackeys were fouling the water. Beetles will crawl from the noses of those lackeys, she said and she meant it, though her word was inadequate.

Suddenly strangers insisted on questions. Why are you standing there, why are you staring? Don't ask me! she rattled, and her men and ladies trembled. What in the fuck do you think you're doing with your life? they asked. Don't ask me! she answered, Don't ask me. All I remember is a blue uniform, a painted pony's tentative legs, green eyes, green hair. Green hair? No, it wasn't green, it was brown, I think. Anyway, it's none of your fucking business, so get the hell out! Tears of gladness grew in all the servants. Daisies danced in the driveways of drunks. All of my life is moon in the morning, moon in the morning, all of my life is moon in the morning, Don't ask me if my mother's alive. Life was hard for her and I hope it's hard for you.

Fantasies of Money

On this beach were every grain a dollar,
every grain a dime, every grain a penny,
and the beach were mine

things would grow under the sand, under my riches,
that would snap for me in the night while I lay there
listening on the strand

to the water making and taking, making, taking,
as if the perpetual cycle of dirt, water, air
promised anything

to the likes of me, or you, or anyone here sleeping
or lying breathlessly awake and dreaming
of missing nothing

most impossible dream of all and last. What lies
under the sand is rising, its jaws sharpen
on the particular

and become it, they sense my drift towards
the dream we share here and the sharers of the dream
near to slipping

into anonymity and particularity as we are tossed
into a perfection that is all we ever truly share
before crashing or drifting back.

Lay

It would need work on the eyes,
I would feel for it and the image
would reach out to me,

peeling off first the military overcoat,
then the sharp glasses, then the Catskills,
then the years of lawful wedding

until my withered grandmother lay white
before me naked and young
and dead and hungry

and that green apple town hugging
itself in snow shrugged its mean thin
shoulders, awful, awful

cutting her deep in where I saw her last
in the bed behind the curtains
of that house that smelled of her.

Sniffed and she was gone. Took off.
The Catskills aching with their growing pains
and those runny brooks of spring.

Reaching out that claw, that claw,
digging up that cruddy factory
and the largemouth waterfall

Where she lay? And reached out?
For a glass of water? Put her
away, wash her away.

A Quiet Scene

The scene that rises
while the dust
settles

on her face
gaunt as the rib-
stretched hide

of a foundered cow
forgotten in autumn
when the boys have run off

deeply to enjoy
their cigarettes beneath
a grey outcrop

beside the swollen slow-
running waters afloat
with leaves and leaves

and leaves of numberless oaks
is more quiet
than that, more

likely to raise up
panic anywhere
small eyes fall

by chance on her,
more a pantomime
of sons' and husband's

irritated sulk
when they find
no supper fuming,

no inevitable heavy
          call come coarse
                as always

from the porch
          to warn the cats
                and dogs about

punctuality in small
          things while the sun
                sticks and scorches

that last intolerable
          sheet stretched over
                the bored Catskills

Doe Day

Sumac mike, red-hackled cock:
I could talk until
I'm knocked up, full
of these refractory Adirondacks:
rummaging in big buck country
for that solitary doe   who will prove me?
listen! Feedback on the Ausable!
You silver listeners full of helgramites,
you birds who watch me stroke my barrel . . .
I'm after the one with the soft nubs,
this special day, babble,
old lightning-rod, current
clattering, tautening with trout.

My voice like threads among the needles,
my voice like trout-sperm in the Ausable,
my voice current among the currents,
sent among the scents, woven
in the waving wish of evergreen,
wish of evergreen, wish of evergreen,
my voice a momentary fish among the evergreens,
a deft bird diving through the Ausable,
voice a red cock strutting among the sorry doe,
voice a bullet slicing through the evergreens,
a wishing through the evergreens
towards heart of doe.

Hard of heart, long among the needles.
My voice a memory among the dead branches.
She will come up from the cold bed of the Ausable,
her eyes swimming in the depths of my wish,
her momentary heart a voice quickening the branches.
She will step out solitary on the grey rock
forehead of the wishful Ausable, she will turn,
cold, on point, on rock, she will turn
to me   and I will take her.

The Price We Pay For The Sun

"We can't go against the law, Dorothy."

Toto is dead now, and
Judy and Bert too, and here
I sit bawling
before the black

and white *put*
him in the basket,
Henry set I borrowed
we've got to get

away, we've got
to run away to watch
these corpses move
we can't do

these things without
reaching out into
the infinite between
the spaghetti commercials.

And I cannot go spinning,
spinning anymore,
up or anywhere,
anymore, the cows

will not blow by
my window anymore,
there will be storms
and storms, but none

will touch me, I will
what's she doing?
Why . . . she's crying
not let them move me.

The very roads themselves
are lost and Glinda
even is no help. Only sit,
that's all, and let the video

kill you. Drop a house
on you. *She's worse
than the other one.*
Drop it. Drop it.

I only want to reach
and scratch his ear
and say beware, beware,
the life in front

of you will kill you,
Judy, Bert, and make
me sad. Just like
the world. Is that

*My! People come
and go so
quickly here!* really
what you want?

We will not go spinning
anymore, we will be still
as scarecrows staring at
(or looking for) the sun.

Rust's echo? *It's too late.
There they are, and there
they'll stay.* Strapped
in a stranger's basket,

trying to make poems of
ruby and gold.

III

Valentine

For The Baby

I

He wanted to feel that
he was making something too
so while she hove and lathered
and gathered in her pulp
he laid a straight line of red
bricks as long as his fatigue
and he said, This is my mother,
look in her eye and think about
some creature that you loved that's dead.

II

She took him backwards, her head
against the wall, her knees spread
and rubbing red, raw against the sheet.
Over her back he saw a small
many-legged being on the wall
looking from two black eyes on nervous stalks
at his own twitching features as he fucked.
He thought, I must remember, before I make some tea,
I must reach and kill it with my shoe.

III

Blue line laid among the gathering cells:
you shall know them by their scars.
What comes forth is everyone's
every time. A wound when it comes
will be like Christmas in spring,
gifts inside gifts. Wound your love
and you will know it when it comes
for what it is, and remember it
when it is empty, lost, or fled.

The Nearly-Dead Children's Ward

It is a grim bar
in Middlefield, CT, called
the Bucket of Blood
and I come in from a twisting drive
whipping my head around
like a zombie on methedrine.

The skills melted in my head.
The long night of my day
shift/rum like sweet kerosene.
Lit up on the lake, the paddleboaters
mooned themselves, drunken sprites
on the boozedamp lilypads.

Where will the summer go? Where
will the summer go? All
the green dancers will whirl around,
turn crisply brown, split and disperse.
When the bartender rings his bell,
some life is ended. When
the dawnlight first reveals
the smudged handprints
the length of the bar-rail,
the juke-box will go up
and the sun go down again.
When I told her my story
about the Nearly-Dead Children's Ward,
she laughed till she nearly cried.

Adios

> *"I'm getting away from things that get bad if I stay. Auspicious beginnings, you know what I mean?"*
> Five Easy Pieces

Time I strip
the walls of my things.
First

to go will be the
clocks, still

there, killing
time. Even to grow
young, in spite
of time, in

spite. But out
of time,

looking in. Look
out. Look
back in

look back in: claw
hammer. Cut
glass. Burnt
umber rug. Crushed
velvet cushion.

Time to stop
stalling. Time
to start, up. And
away, a way. Where

bare walls bear
all the weight, bare
all, bear all
the wait away.

Poem To Be Recited While Wheeling My Mother Through The University

The moon is moving north
on I-32 at sixty-five MPH
with a wizened brown woman at the wheel.

In Syracuse or Ithaca the sleek yellow door
opens to take on a pale rider,
quick, quick, quick to cop a feel

from my mother there, my dour
grandmother, my fantastic queer
woman-in-the-moon, the real

villain of every driving-nightmare,
the certain wrecker of every dreamcar,
the quizzical one withering in the bawdy tale.

Sycamore Song

Past where
the sycamore
is an adolescent dancer
fighting off hornets

who slings the morning
sparrows deep against
the sky
I would fly

grotesque bird
of the crepuscule
flapping towards the dark
and cry after cry.

The wings with their myriad
parasites creak and molt.
My voice, my song: a cackle
harrowing the ones left
crippled in the afternoon.

My long green tongue
which sees itself
flaps like a third wing
and is meaningless.

Past the sun
past moonlight
past the white lies
of those little pricks
the stars

I flap to find
a perfect blackness
there to lose this

where the dance of light
and objects goes
to roost or dies
or shuts its many traps

and the mirror at my lips
no my beak
refuses to give
anything back.

Ambiguous Birds

What is this thing, copper
and metal-flake, picking the gravel
driveway for my father's seed?

He keeps them in the woods
as emblems to confirm each morning:
wonder of simple regularity,

like the gay fluttering
of the tiny bird in the pulse
just at the heart's last buck:

they come when you most
expect them. What thing
is this, red around the eyes

and unable to eat
for croaking? Must be
the poet-bird, nut-bird, duck-

the-world bird. A plain
grey sparrow comes with such a rush
of crimson at its neck

that my father is crying.
"All the little bee-bees,"
he babbles, "find their little throats."

But it is only a Blood-Throated
Something-or-other, gulping
down his seed to dump it back

there in the woods. It is not
really my mother, the tired bird
of the tireless lymphoma.

And the great circles
in the air around it all,
those invisible harmonies

of circumference, is that
a hawk high up, and what
will he carry to his nest today?

The Caterpillar-Song

In spring when we
take it out
comes puzzled the bearded
caterpillar
dragging it through
the old field
of revision, on an old shore where
there are wells
on every hill, full
of frogs
and nostalgia. The soft
caterpillar
stiffens in the sun. We
take it when
we want it if we want it,
but we aren't
sure we want it. There are
plank shacks
in every old oak, full
of ants and
avuncular yellowjackets.
We must take
those fortresses, where the tent
caterpillars
pitch themselves over
the high sea,
the fish-mouths gaping under.
When they bite,
we take them with one
sharp tug,
setting the barb deep in the soft
lip of the old
fish resentfully dying. We
take it
if it is big enough, old

enough, if it's
legal and approved and sure
to be too tough
to be useful, when we take it
it is already wasted.
There are strong men with
crewcuts and blue
riding-breeches with red
racing-stripes mounted
on painted stallions in every
flowered park,
to take pictures of, shitting
on the dahlias,
while the harried caterpillar
hustles from dropping
to dropping, sniffing here,
ducking there, chewing
now and now eschewing, until
in a flash of
passion or insight or boredom
or wit or malice
or strategy or intoxication
or infatuation or
anger or mischievousness or
poetry or samsara
or prestidigitation or flatulence
or metamorphosis
he takes it: and burrowing through
that old dung-ball
he sings the caterpillar-song,
which goes:
caterpillar pater-killer
caterpillar pater-killer
caterpillar pater-killer
caterpillar pater-killer
caterpillar pater-killer
caterpillar pater-killer
caterpillar pater-killer

caterpillar pater-killer, etc.,
until he can't sing it anymore
whether from
laughing or crying and then
for a short while
he will be or appear to be
something or someone else,
and we take it, and we
put our pin through it
to try to make it last forever.

" 'That One Should Stand In An Aquarium' "

They buy my father
                an aquarium
now every night
                they say
he sits and fiddles
                with the dials
contrast   brightness   horizontal
                squinting saying
is the color right yet
                is that clear

now staring not talking
                moves the antenna
to turn a neon tetra to
                clear blue somewhere
I am willing myself
                into that tank
one day he may switch
                channels to wonder
again at the churning fighting
                fishes' dance and
I will appear
                my lips
moving up the side
                of the tank
bubbling up turn
                it off turn it off

will he bring himself
                to that channel
before he finds the deep one
                where puzzled and scared
he will try to stop the lazy revolutions
                to recognize the flat eyes
of that buried patient holy
                roller his
stepmother and the
                power breaks?

Spring Frogs In Late Winter

Something so hot
they were out in millions today
wriggling out of thick mud
bubbled through the puddles
in the back field, really
a wine-bottle-bothered lot.

Local boys hunt-glowed
sharpened sumac sticks
pale little bushmen
darting from bush to bush
beat the puddles until they hop
looking for tall grass.

At first it's a stand-off,
see who gets the first one,
nobody got none.
They whipped their long needle sticks
into the short grass
never killed a one.

So soon enough
they moved in close
and jabbed them one by one,
like park attendants
spearing their paychecks
off immaculate lawns

imagining their fathers'
faces in the grass.

Song

The father of the one I love
has herself made something beautiful,
a poem, a picture, some bright thing—
and this I can love with no fear.

He makes her swans
fat dogs
rolling on clear green water

He makes her goblets
two-faced
blue in the mouth

He instructs her servants
join in song for me
I am melancholy

He collects his thoughts
about accounting
and sells millions

All of the loves of my love's father
carry sleek gigolos on expense accounts
she smiles on them all, my Buddha,
cringes at anyone's least discomfort.

There are pens
inscribed with her name
stuck in my wall

he makes her gentlemen
to holler
like hog-callers

he wishes

fine silks for the beds
of my broken parents

under her floorboards
box upon box
of cold tin soldiers

This is the song of my love's father
she made me put down
she made me put down
just before the candle ate itself.

Shut Up

They're always saying stupid
stupid. Stupid. Why
don't you shut up those
hypocrites O I hate.

Take a shower in a dump
hotel and right across
the wall they're banging
stop that stupid singing
stupid.

I get up before dawn
and out the window down
the pipe to the alley
creep to the back among
the clutter bring my voice
way up like a girl's or cat's
they all scream hey
shut up! shut up!

Up at my father's farm
where the partridges sing
with their wings pigs
sing with twisted tails cows
with heavy eyes the last
elm with its Dutch blight
I only want to sing
they stop me stupid shut up.

At my mother's lying-in
I couldn't quite touch
her I sang like a baby
laughing I put my
tears on her singing
my father was on fire.

They always watch
I only wanted to
sing I am and will be
stupid as the daylight
I will shut up
if I can only sing.
The voices of the worst
of them are singing
shut up shut up they sing.

Getting On / Empty Set

Would, have tried to,
be just
what you're looking through
or to for something

There are the tiny
ones that swim upon the air
and there is a small
gift for you, there, there

You have sat and watched
me, now, so what
did you expect, one more
gesture, more words,

more gestures, more words,
when somebody clearheaded, smart,
somewhere has probably clearly shown
that all of these are empty?

*

There will be
a clock, but
no anticipation, there

will be a rowboat,
dad,
but neither oars nor anchor.

Let it all go
where it will
go, understand

with me the over-

hang of this moment
our lives make

I, you
standing
under it

but looking out and
through, for,
forever over

where the big ones
swim this mud creek
emptied of its own turnings.

*

Now they are running in
        my arms, those
              agents of the
                  cartoon emperor

All righteethen, All
        righteethen is what
              they say like cowpokes
                    to each other

They work by contraction,
        by contracting, by
              contract in
                    all the joints

The strip is full of them
        when I stand
              emptied, as
                    always

They can't tell me

what to do, says
    each of them of
        all the others

I can still slice
    that wrist and dump
        them cleanly down
            the sink

*

Waiting for Bardot
would be the name
of the movie I would write
for you, simple-

ton of my dreaming,
tagalong, doughnut.
We'd play all the parts,
including yardstick,

harpsichord, billy-goat,
aging professor, that pig
mayor of Philadelphia,
and Brigitte herself,

who never appears on screen,
and we would play
the screen as well, and you
could be the projector.

*

I would build a set of nothing
made of nothing and resembling
nothing. I would nail it down
to nothing with nothing.

I would climb that set, careful
not to fall or stub my toe,
careful of footholds, wary of
everything. I would get high

up on that set, until nothing
impeded my view of those
absent eyes before me. Would
I cry or laugh? How

do you improve on nothing?
No script! Even a blank page
would be too much. Just
a feather on the stage,

and down I'd crash, bump
my head on something, and arise
a writhing image of myselves, hard-
ly visible, hardly evanesced at all.

for Robert Creeley

Dream Of Stuyvesant Falls, 1954, 1959, And 1962

Appalling dialect: greenery trumped.
Wagged tongue of nightmare dangles,
used up. Understand? Bushes
upon bushes full of familial faces
looking over my shoulder while the dead grocer's
son who now owns racinghorses in Houston
teaches me twelve-card-stud the "hard" way.
Up there where an apple should be,
in clear view but out of reach,
my skinny egg-headed cousin,
out of my life for twenty years, wears
a red psychotic agon-mask
from the Greek drama. His scream
is like a cat being castrated
by a dog: Go for it! Ai-yee!
Go ahead and try for it! Mike
turns over my hand, pulls out the sore thumb
ace, swallows my life savings and drawls
with someone else's voice, almost a woman's voice,
rule three: never draw to the inside straight.
Next he and I are pissing on the bushes.

"Cultivate And Make Music"

"The dream was bidding me to do what I was already doing, in the same way that the competitor in a race is bidden by the spectators to run when he is already running."

Socrates on the day of his
death, in *Phaedo*

Not running but dancing
in a minefield, the fans
moaning softly, together, blow,
blow, blow, blow. Meaning
I am sorry that your head
hurts you so. Let us forget
it together. Many blessings
will not rhyme, will not compute,
will not execute. The fans
say touch, touch, touch the one
next to me, let me watch.
Each of us ready to go off,
for Hecuba? For Socrates?
For that little headless boy
in Florida? The fans
cry out O no, no, no,
no fair to bring that up.
Just dance, dream, go on,
do what you were already doing,
that was fine, just don't blow
up until you hit the mine.

Cold

It is not you, it is not you,
they say when they speak at all,
our voices through the night.
I know the time is odd out there,
and people say *Right on*
and do not fear earthquakes
spilling them in the pacific.
It is *cold* here, cold
of distances and electric contacts.
The possum who visits me
with his rodent face oblivious
at my window has not come tonight:
too cold perhaps. I am open
inside, like an empty saloon.
It is cold in there. Only
possums line up at that bar,
and no one ever answers anything
right, the jukebox plays
a dull television voice:
In L.A. no one died tonight
in a small shock and smaller
aftershock, and no one cared
and no one spoke, but it was warm
and your face came on but I
think I missed it.

Springsong For My Parents

The breathless constellations
hardly nod as eternity passes:
They keep no watch,
they've pulled the stops from time.
All those endless children,
their cells proliferating,
openly retreat to jetties,
runways, lightless golf greens.
The blood-tanager
hellos his beloved
out of black bushes.
Peepers chime their childhood up,
silver bells, bells.

The moon is Hoagy Carmichael,
and the stars are just crooning.

Valentine

My love you are to me
like the pecker on a Samoan idol
by which I mean
I have never truly seen beneath
that stone you wear for pride

and I invent and then
invent you yet again and I
am ready to invent you
till you come clean
and honest and open

like an oyster
or like a door marked
*Clean. Honest. Open
Me*, but there's again
that stone wall right behind.

Or there's a door
behind the door behind
the door behind etc., each
an eye which opens, squeaking
I'm I, I'm I,

each a lie
carved from the deeper
lie of stone,
the hard, ardent, hardened one
we carve our two hearts upon.